Jill and the Giant Spill

Anders Hanson

Consulting Editor, Diane Craig, M.A./Reading Specialist

Published by ABDO Publishing Company, 4940 Viking Drive, Edina, Minnesota 55435.

Printed in the United States.

Credits
Edited by: Pam Price
Curriculum Coordinator: Nancy Tuminelly
Cover and Interior Design and Production: Mighty Media
Photo Credits: AbleStock, Corbis Images, Digital Vision, Anders Hanson, Tracy Kompelien

Library of Congress Cataloging-in-Publication Data

Hanson, Anders, 1980-
    Jill and the giant spill / Anders Hanson.
        p. cm. -- (First rhymes)
    Includes index.
    ISBN 1-59679-491-7 (hardcover)
    ISBN 1-59679-492-5 (paperback)
        1. English language--Rhyme--Juvenile literature. I. Title. II. Series.
PE1517.H37544 2005
808.1--dc22
                                                                                2005048551

SandCastle™ books are created by a professional team of educators, reading specialists, and content developers around five essential components that include phonemic awareness, phonics, vocabulary, text comprehension, and fluency. All books are written, reviewed, and leveled for guided reading and early intervention reading, and designed for use in shared, guided, and independent reading and writing activities to support a balanced approach to literacy instruction.

Let Us Know

After reading the book, SandCastle would like you to tell us your stories about reading. What is your favorite page? Was there something hard that you needed help with? Share the ups and downs of learning to read. We want to hear from you! To get posted on the ABDO Publishing Company Web site, send us e-mail at:

sandcastle@abdopub.com

SandCastle Level: Beginning

-ill

hill

ill

mill

quill

spill

I see the  .

He is  .

Here is a 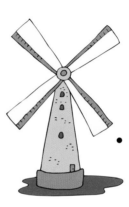.

We look at a .

We see the  .

The hill is tall.

Rick feels ill.

The mill is big.

The quill is long.

The spill is messy.

Jill and the Giant Spill

A giant named Jill
lives on top of a hill.

On top of Jill's hill
is a mill.

Inside the mill
on the hill,
Jill writes with
ink and quill.

"Today I feel ill," writes Jill on the hill with her quill.

Jill is so ill
that she sneezes
on the quill
and makes the ink spill
out of the mill
and down the hill.

About SandCastle™

A professional team of educators, reading specialists, and content developers created the SandCastle™ series to support young readers as they develop reading skills and strategies and increase their general knowledge. The SandCastle™ series has four levels that correspond to early literacy development in young children. The levels are provided to help teachers and parents select the appropriate books for young readers.

Emerging Readers
(no flags)

Beginning Readers
(1 flag)

Transitional Readers
(2 flags)

Fluent Readers
(3 flags)

These levels are meant only as a guide. All levels are subject to change.

ABDO
Publishing Company

To see a complete list of SandCastle™ books and other nonfiction titles from ABDO Publishing Company, visit **www.abdopub.com** or contact us at:
4940 Viking Drive, Edina, Minnesota 55435 • 1-800-800-1312 • fax: 1-952-831-1632